Oxford **A-Z**
of **English Usage**

Second Edition

Editor
Jeremy Butterfield

OXFORD
UNIVERSITY PRESS

OXFORD
UNIVERSITY PRESS

Great Clarendon Street, Oxford, OX2 6DP,
United Kingdom

Oxford University Press is a department of the University of Oxford.
It furthers the University's objective of excellence in research, scholarship,
and education by publishing worldwide. Oxford is a registered trade mark of
Oxford University Press in the UK and in certain other countries

© Oxford University Press 2007, 2013

The moral rights of the author have been asserted

First Edition published in 2007
Second Edition published in 2013

Impression: 1

British Library Cataloguing in Publication Data
Data available

Library of Congress Cataloging in Publication Data
Data available

Printed in Great Britain by
Ashford Colour Press Ltd, Gosport, Hampshire

ISBN 978-0-19-965245-7

Contents

Key to pronunciations

....

The pronunciation of a word, when necessary, is given by respelling it, and it is shown between forward slashes (e.g. '**Adult** is usually pronounced /**ad**-ult/ in British English'). This system is very easy to follow, but a few symbols need explanation:

a   the vowel sound in 'cat'

I   the sound of the word 'eye'

i   the vowel sound in 'kid'

oo   the vowel sound in 'root'

ow   the vowel sound in 'cow'

th   the 'hard th' in 'thick'

th   the 'soft th' in 'this'

uu   the vowel sound in 'book'

uh   the sound of the 'a' in 'along'

'   a hint of an /uh/ sound, as in /**foh**-k'l/ 'focal'

Preface

The *Oxford A-Z of English Usage* offers straightforward, up-to-date guidance on questions of English usage, some very familiar to many readers, some probably not so familiar, but all affecting the language we choose and how effectively we get our message across.

The advice and information given are based on analysis of the Oxford English Corpus, a database containing more than two billion words of real 21st-century English, collected from a huge variety of sources. The entries therefore reflect modern practice and attitudes, revealing, for example, how *straight-laced* is now actually used more commonly than the traditional spelling *strait-laced*. The entries are also illustrated with examples of real English drawn from the Corpus.

Common confusions such as *uninterested* and *disinterested* are explained, differences between British and American practice are highlighted, and a realistic attitude is taken towards famous examples such as splitting infinitives, ending a sentence with a preposition, and when it is correct to say *you and me* or *you and I*.

Longer articles allow discussion of wider points, such as the dramatic changes that have occurred in English in recent years through attempts to use 'gender-neutral' language, and why it is important to use hyphens correctly in some contexts, while it makes little difference whether many compounds are written with a hyphen or not.

Thanks to Oxford's unique resources, this book simultaneously reflects real, modern English usage and makes use of the expertise and authority for which Oxford Dictionaries are world-famous. To explore the language further try Oxford Dictionaries Online. This free site is updated regularly and allows you to search the *Oxford Dictionary of English* and its US counterpart, the *New Oxford American Dictionary*. It also offers information on usage, grammar, and writing, Word of the Day, and a language blog. The subscription-based Oxford Dictionaries Pro features linked, fully searchable dictionaries and thesauruses, audio pronunciations, millions of example sentences, and specialist language reference resources. Find Oxford Dictionaries Online at www.oxforddictionaries.com.

a, an

A and **an** are the two forms of 'the indefinite article'. See AN for information on which to use before

- words beginning with **h**, e.g. *hotel*
- words beginning with a letter that is normally a vowel, e.g. *unique*
- initialisms, e.g. *SAS*

abbreviations

People are often unsure about these questions to do with abbreviations:

- whether to write them with capital letters
- which ones need full stops
- when to use apostrophes

There are four main kinds of abbreviation: shortenings, contractions, initialisms, and acronyms. Standard practice depends on the kind of abbreviation in question.

1 Shortenings are abbreviations where the beginning or end of the word has been dropped: *cello* = violoncello, *flu* = influenza, *ad* = advertisement, *bike* = bicycle, *pub* = public house, *rhino* = rhinoceros, *telly* = television. In some cases the longer form is only used in technical or formal writing and could sound quaint or affected in speech.

- Because such shortenings are now an accepted part of the language, you no longer need to put an apostrophe at the beginning or end.

- Where the shortening is only ever written, such as *Dec.* = December, *Tue.* = Tuesday, or *etc.* = et cetera, a full stop is used.

2 Contractions are a type of abbreviation in which letters from the middle of the word are omitted: *Dr* = Doctor, *St* = Saint, *Ltd* = Limited.

▶

- Because the last letter of the word is present, no full stop is used: *Dr*, *Revd*, *Mrs*.

- In verb forms and archaic words, the omitted letters are replaced by an apostrophe: *can't* = cannot, *we've* = we have; *ne'er-do-well* = never-do-well, *o'er* = over.

3 **Initialisms** are abbreviations which consist of the initial letters of words and which are pronounced as separate letters: *a.m., BBC, MOD, MP, QC, UN, TUC*.

- British style is not to include full stops, whereas American style tends to.

- The plural is formed by adding an **-s**, now normally without an apostrophe (e.g. *MPs* and *QCs* rather than *MP's* or *QC's*). Possessives are formed in the usual way (e.g. *an MP's salary*; *several MPs' secretaries*).

4 **Acronyms** are words formed from the initial letters of other words, and pronounced as they are spelled: *Aids, NATO*. Some of them, such as *radar* and *laser*, have become normal words.

- They can be written all as capitals or only with an initial capital, and house styles vary. With some words, such as *Aids*, there is a tendency to have only an initial capital.

able-bodied, abled

It is best to avoid using **able-bodied** to mean 'not having a physical disability', since many people with disabilities object to its use in this way. Their preferred word is **non-disabled**. **Abled**, meaning 'not disabled', is a revival of an obsolete 16th-century word, and has been recorded in print in the US since the 1980s. It is now used in the phrase **differently abled** as a more positive alternative to **disabled**.

Aboriginal, Aborigine

Australian **Aborigines** prefer to be known as **Indigenous Australians**, and this phrase is becoming more and more standard. While both **Aboriginal** and **Aborigine** may be used as nouns, **Aborigine** is the commoner and preferred choice. **Aboriginal** is the term used by the Australian government, but is disliked by **Indigenous Australians** themselves.

abstruse

For the confusion between **abstruse** and **obtuse**, see OBTUSE.

access

The verb **to access** is standard and common in computing and related terminology. But its use outside computing contexts, although well established, is sometimes criticized as being 'jargon': *you must use a password to access the account*. If you want an alternative, you could use a word or phrase such as 'enter' or 'gain access to': *to gain access to the information*. For more information on formations of this kind, see VERBS FORMED FROM NOUNS.

accusative, accusatory

Accusative is a grammatical term referring to the grammatical case of the object of a verb. Using it to mean 'accusing', as in *an accusative tone*, is incorrect. The correct word is **accusatory**: *turning on his heel, he pointed an accusatory finger at von Laffeyhosen*.

acknowledgement

The spelling with **-dge-** is more common in all varieties of English than the spelling with **-dg-**, though both are correct. British English tends to prefer the form with **-dge-**.

AD

AD is normally written in small capital letters and should be placed before the numerals, as in AD *375* (not *375* AD). This is because AD is an abbreviation of *anno domini*, which means 'in the year of our Lord', and should logically come before the year. However, it is normal to write *the third century*

AD (not AD *the third century*). AD is written without full stops after the letters. See also BC.

addenda, addendum

Addenda is a Latin plural form meaning 'a list of additional items'. If there is only one item, **addendum** is the correct traditional form to use. **Addenda** should therefore only ever be used as a plural, not as a singular. So, you may well be thought wrong if you use **addenda** as a singular, as in *a new edition with an invaluable addenda*, instead of the correct *a new edition with invaluable addenda*. Worse still is to use the non-existent plural *addendas*. See also LATIN PLURALS.

address

The verb **address**, although it seems at first glance to promise forceful action, can justifiably be criticized for being overused. Moreover, when someone undertakes to *address an issue* it is often unclear to what exactly they are committing. Will they merely note it as something to be dealt with at an unspecified future date, analyse it in depth, or actually resolve it as soon as humanly possible? To avoid what some people regard as a bit of a woolly cliché, it may be better to specify the exact measures you intend taking. Or else use **resolve**, **deal with**, or **sort out** instead.

admission, admittance

Admission traditionally referred to the price paid for entry or the right to enter: *admission was £5*. **Admittance** more often referred to physical entry: *we were denied admittance by a large man with a forbidding scowl*. In this meaning of 'permission or right to enter', these words have become almost interchangeable, although **admittance** is more formal and technical.

ad nauseam

The correct spelling of this Latin phrase is with **-eam** at the end. Some people write it with **-eum**, perhaps influenced by the fact that the phrase *ad infinitum* ends in **-um**. Whatever the reason for the mistake, if you go to the trouble of using a Latin phrase in the first place, it is best to write it correctly.

adult

The standard way to pronounce **adult** in British English is to emphasize the first syllable: /**ad**-ult/. Emphasizing the second syllable, /uh-**dult**/, is an alternative, and is the standard for speakers of American English. This pronunciation is becoming more widespread in British English, and, though many people dislike it, is acceptable. Interestingly, in 1884 the *Oxford English Dictionary* suggested the second pronunciation as the preferred version.

adversary

The standard way to pronounce **adversary** in British English is to emphasize the first syllable only: /**ad**-ver-suh-ree/. Speakers of American English add a secondary stress before the third syllable, which they also pronounce differently: /**ad**-ver-**sai**-ree/.

adverse

Adverse and **averse** are related in origin but mean different things. **Adverse** means 'unfavourable or harmful' and is normally used of conditions and effects rather than people, as in *adverse weather conditions*. **Averse**, on the other hand, is used of people (nearly always followed by **to**), and means 'having a strong dislike or opposition to something', as in *I am not averse to helping out*. A common mistake is to use **adverse** instead of **averse**, as in *he is not adverse to making a profit*.

advertise

Advertise is correctly spelled *-ise*, never *-ize*.

adviser, advisor

The spelling **advisor** is about half as common as **adviser**. More common in North America than in Britain, it is a more recent development and is still regarded by some people as incorrect.

a

affect

Affect and **effect** are quite different in meaning, though frequently confused. **Affect** is primarily a verb meaning 'make a difference to', as in *their gender need not affect their career*. **Effect**, on the other hand, is used both as a noun and a verb, meaning 'a result' as a noun (*move the cursor until you get the effect you want*) or 'to bring about a result' as a verb (*growth in the economy can only be effected by stringent economic controls*). The two verbs have very similar meanings, so it often pays to think carefully which one you want.

African American, Afro-American

African American is the currently accepted term in the US for Americans of African origin, having first become prominent in the late 1980s. it has largely replaced **Afro-American**, which was first recorded in the 19th century and became widespread in the 1960s and 1970s. In Britain, **black** is the standard term.

afterward, afterwards

Afterward is a standard form only in US English, but it is still outnumbered two to one by **afterwards** in the American writing in the Oxford English Corpus. In all other varieties of English, **afterwards** is the only customary form.

agenda

Though **agenda** is the plural of **agendum** in Latin, in standard modern English it is normally used as a singular noun. It therefore has a standard English plural form: **agendas**, not *'agendae'*, as is sometimes seen.

aggravate

Aggravate in the sense 'to annoy or exasperate' dates back to the 17th century and has been so used by respected writers ever since. This use is still regarded as incorrect by some traditionalists on the grounds that it is too radical a departure from the etymological meaning of 'to make heavy'. It is, however, comparable to meaning changes in hundreds of other words which have long been accepted without comment.

ago

When **ago** is followed by a clause, the clause should be introduced by **that** rather than **since**, e.g. *it was sixty years ago that I left this place*, but you could avoid **ago** by writing *it is sixty years since I left this place*.

agreement

Agreement (also called *concord*) is the correct relation of different parts of a sentence to each other: for example, the form of a verb should correspond to its subject: *the* **house was** *small, and its* **walls were** *painted white*; again, the gender and number (singular or plural) of a pronoun should conform to those of the person or thing it refers to: *he had never been close enough to a* **girl** *to consider making* **her** *his wife*. As English has lost many inflections over centuries of use, problems of agreement only arise in the two cases just mentioned. This article deals with noun-verb agreement. Discussion of pronoun agreement and other aspects of verb agreement is dealt with under individual entries: see AND, ANY, AS WELL AS, EACH, EITHER, GENDER-NEUTRAL LANGUAGE, HALF, KIND, NONE, NUMBER, OR, SORT, and THEY. Here are some typical difficulties that people have in making verbs agree with noun subjects.

1 Sentences, especially long ones, in which the verb is separated from its singular subject by intervening words in the plural can make the speaker or writer put the verb in the plural, but these examples are incorrect: *the* **consequence** *of long periods of inactivity or situations in which patients cannot look after themselves* **are** *often quite severe and long-lasting*; **copyright** *of Vivienne's papers* **are** *in the keeping of the Haigh-Wood family*.
In the first example there are three options: ▶

change *consequence* to *consequences*, change *are* to *is*, or (probably best) recast the sentence more simply, *e.g. Long periods of inactivity... can often have quite severe and long-lasting consequences.*

2 Two nouns joined by **and**: these normally form a plural subject and require a plural verb: *speed and accuracy are what is needed*; *fish and chips are served in the evening.* But when the noun phrase is regarded as a singular unit, it can take a singular verb: *fish and chips is my favourite meal*; *wine, women, and song was the leitmotiv of his lifestyle.* This can extend to concepts that are distinct in themselves but are regarded as a single item in a particular sentence: *a certain cynicism and resignation comes along with advancing years.*

The last convention is very old, with evidence dating back to Old and Middle English. Clearly there will be borderline cases, and then it is what sounds natural that matters: ***the hurt and disbelief** of parents' friends and families **is/are** already quite real.*

3 Two or more nouns can be joined by words other than **and**, e.g. *accompanied by, as well as, not to mention, together with*, etc. These noun groups are followed by a singular verb if the first noun or noun phrase is singular, because the addition is not regarded as part of the grammatical subject: *even such a very profitable company, along with many other companies in the UK, **is** not prepared to pay even a reasonable amount*; *Daddy had on the hairy tweed **jacket** with leather elbow patches which, together with his pipe, **was** his trademark.*

4 When a subject and a complement of different number (singular/plural) are separated by the verb *to be* (or verbs such as *become, seem*, etc.), the verb should agree with the number of the subject, not that of the complement:

- (singular subject and plural complement) *the only **traffic** **is** ox-carts and bicycles*; *the **view** it obscured **was** pipes, fire escapes, and a sooty wall* ▶

- (plural subject and singular complement) *the socials were a big deal to her*; *the March events were a natural stage in the evolution of democracy in the country*.

  NB: There are some exceptions, depending on the meaning in particular cases: *more nurses* (i.e. the topic of more nurses) *is the next item on the agenda*.

albeit

1 **Albeit** is not an archaic word, although it may sound like one. It is used as a conjunction with the meaning 'though', to make a contrast with or to modify a preceding expression: *it is an unwelcome, albeit necessary, piece of legislation*.

2 It should not be written as the three words 'all be it' in modern Standard English.

3 Even though most conjunctions are used with verbs, e.g. *you just keep going because you have no choice*, it is not good style to use **albeit** with a verb, as in *Mr Gaunt is as culpable as the others, albeit he was not involved in any of the incidents*. The explanation for this is that **albeit** derived from the phrase 'all be it that', which already contained a verb.

alibi

The word **alibi**, which in Latin means 'elsewhere', has been used since the 18th century to mean 'an assertion by a person that he or she was elsewhere'. In the 20th century a new meaning arose, originally in the US, of 'an excuse'. This is a fairly common and natural extension of the core meaning, but, though widely accepted in standard English, it is still regarded as incorrect by some people.

alright

There is no logical reason for insisting that **alright** is incorrect and should always be written as **all right**, when other single-word forms such as **altogether** have long been accepted. The fact that **alright** is not recorded until the end of the

a

19th century, while other similar merged spellings such as
altogether and **already** date from much earlier, is no reason for
denouncing it, but many people still find it unacceptable in
formal writing.

alternative

The adjective **alternate** is sometimes used in place of
alternative, especially in American English. In British English the
two words continue to be quite distinct: **alternative** means
'available as another possibility or choice', as in *some European
countries follow an alternative approach*. **Alternate** means 'every
other', as in *they meet on alternate Sundays*, or 'each following
the other in a regular pattern', as in *alternate layers of potato and
sauce*. The use of **alternate** to mean **alternative**, as in *we will
need to find alternate sources of fuel*, is common in North America,
and many US dictionaries now record it as equivalent in this
meaning to **alternative**. In British English, however, it is not
yet considered good style.

although

The form **although** can be replaced by **though**, the only
difference being that **although** tends to be more formal than
though.

altogether

Note that **altogether** and **all together** do not mean the same
thing. **Altogether** means 'in total', as in *there are six bedrooms
altogether*, whereas **all together** means 'all in one place' or 'all at
once', as in *it was good to have a group of friends all together; they
came in all together*.

alumnus

Alumnus comes from Latin, and refers to an ex-student of a
particular university or similar educational establishment.
The plural is **alumni**. The technically correct form for a female
ex-student is **alumna**, the plural of which is **alumnae**. **Alumni** is
the form to use when referring to groups including both sexes,
and **alumnae** when they are exclusively female. Although